IT'S TIME TO EAT STRAWBERRIES

It's Time to Eat STRAWBERRIES

Walter the Educator

Silent King Books
A WhichHead Entertainment Imprint

Copyright © 2024 by Walter the Educator

All rights reserved. No part of this book may be reproduced in any manner whatsoever without written per- mission except in the case of brief quotations embodied in critical articles and reviews.

First Printing, 2024

Disclaimer

This book is a literary work; the story is not about specific persons, locations, situations, and/or circumstances unless mentioned in a historical context. Any resemblance to real persons, locations, situations, and/or circumstances is coincidental. This book is for entertainment and informational purposes only. The author and publisher offer this information without warranties expressed or implied. No matter the grounds, neither the author nor the publisher will be accountable for any losses, injuries, or other damages caused by the reader's use of this book. The use of this book acknowledges an understanding and acceptance of this disclaimer.

It's Time to Eat STRAWBERRIES is a collectible early learning book by Walter the Educator suitable for all ages belonging to Walter the Educator's Time to Eat Book Series. Collect more books at WaltertheEducator.com

USE THE EXTRA SPACE TO TAKE NOTES AND DOCUMENT YOUR MEMORIES

STRAWBERRIES

It's snack time now, come take a look,

It's Time to Eat
Strawberries

What's in the basket or on the cook?

It's red and shiny, sweet as can be,

Hooray for strawberries, just for me!

They grow on plants so green and low,

In sunny fields, where soft winds blow.

Pick them fresh or buy a bunch,

Strawberries make the perfect munch!

Hold one close, it smells so sweet,

A fruity snack that's hard to beat.

Take a bite, it's juicy and bright,

Strawberries bring such pure delight!

With seeds on the outside, tiny and neat,

They add some crunch to every treat.

Soft and tender, they melt away,

Strawberries make a better day.

It's Time to Eat
Strawberries

Dip them in chocolate, or whipped cream too,

Strawberries have so much to do!

Add them to yogurt, cakes, or pie,

Or eat them plain, they'll make you sigh.

Some are big, and some are small,

Some are round, some not at all.

No matter the size, they're always sweet,

Strawberries are the perfect treat.

A little tart, a little sweet,

They're a snack that can't be beat.

Healthy, yummy, so much fun,

Strawberries shine beneath the sun.

Share them with friends or eat them alone,

Strawberries make you feel at home.

A bowl of red, so bright and cheery,

It's Time to Eat
Strawberries

This fruity snack will keep you merry!

So every time you see their glow,

Pick a strawberry, let the fun grow.

Snack time's here, it's simply the best,

Strawberries beat all the rest!

Now clap and cheer, hooray, hooray,

For strawberries brighten every day!

With every bite, they bring a smile,

It's Time to Eat
Strawberries

Making snack time so worthwhile.

ABOUT THE CREATOR

Walter the Educator is one of the pseudonyms for Walter Anderson. Formally educated in Chemistry, Business, and Education, he is an educator, an author, a diverse entrepreneur, and he is the son of a disabled war veteran. "Walter the Educator" shares his time between educating and creating. He holds interests and owns several creative projects that entertain, enlighten, enhance, and educate, hoping to inspire and motivate you. Follow, find new works, and stay up to date with Walter the Educator™

at WaltertheEducator.com

www.ingramcontent.com/pod-product-compliance
Lightning Source LLC
LaVergne TN
LVHW010411070526
838199LV00064B/5262